WO
FORCES
TO BE
RECKONED
WITH
Formidable Men
Jewel Hampton

WORKBOOK

FORCES TO BE RECKONED WITH FORMIDABLE MEN

Copyright © 2023 Jewel Hampton

All rights reserved. No part of this book may be reproduced or transmitted in any form or by any means without written permission from the author.

ISBN: 979-8-9891228-3-7

Printed in the USA

All Scripture quotations are taken from the King James Bible Version.

Cover design: Jewel Hampton

Graphics licensed from Shutterstock

WORKBOOK DEDICATION

This book is dedicated to every man who yearns for more knowledge of God's word. May studying the lives of other men who overcame struggles and obstacles help to illuminate your path, inspire you to greatness, and strengthen your walk in Christ.

CONTENTS

1.	Adam	1
2.	Noah	4
3	Enoch	7
4.	Abraham	10
5.	Isaac	13
6.	Jacob	16
7.	Joseph	21
8.	Judah	24
9.	Moses	27
10.	Aaron	31
11.	Joshua	34
12.	Caleb	37
13.	Samson	40
14.	Samuel	43
15.	David	48
16.	Elijah	51
17.	Jonadab	55
18.	Job	58

19.	Daniel	63
20.	The Three Hebrew Boys	67
21.	Zacharias	70
22.	Joseph of Nazareth	73
23.	Simeon	76
24.	John the Baptist	78
25.	The Apostles	81
26.	Nicodemus	85
27.	The Nobleman	87
28.	The Roman Centurion	89
29.	Jairus	91
30.	Zacchaeus	93
31.	Stephen	95
32.	Philip	99
33	Paul	102

INTRODUCTION

This is the companion workbook to the book "Forces to be Reckoned With: Formidable Men." The key to this book is to study it alongside the book and/or with your Bible.

Scripture references are in parenthesis and are quoted from the King James Version. References to a page number in the book are preceded with a P (i.e., P48 would be page 48 in the book).

3. God formed man from the dust of the ground. What did he do that man became "a living soul?" (Genesis 2:7) P2

4. Where did God plant the garden where he put man? (Genesis 2:8) P2

5. What was the man to do in the garden? (Genesis 2:15) P2

6. What tree was man not to eat of in the garden? (Genesis 2:17) P2

7. What would happen to the man on the day he ate of that tree? (Genesis 2:17) P2

8. How was the woman formed? (Genesis 2:21-22) P2

9. Why do you think Adam and Eve were unashamed of being unclothed?

10. How did all mankind sin as a result of Adam and Eve's sin? (Romans 5:10) P3

11. What hope was given that there would be a future redeemer? (Genesis 3:15) P3

12. What did God place before the garden to prevent Adam and Eve from re-entering? (Genesis 3:24) P3

***Thought question.** Eve ate of the deadly tree first, but Adam was standing with her and did not refuse the food. Do you think he considered God had said don't eat of the tree, but ate because his wife gave it to him? Have there been times you can recall when you did something you knew was wrong?*

2 NOAH

1. Fill in the blank. (Genesis 6:8 KJV) P6

    But Noah found __GRACE__ in the eyes of the LORD.

2. Circle the correct answer. (Genesis 6:9) P6

    Noah was _found upright & full of integrity_

    a) a just man

    b) perfect in his generations

    (c) both)

3. How many sons did Noah have?

    Three

4. What were the names of Noah's sons? (Genesis 6:10) P6

Shem, Ham, Japheth

5. Why was God going to destroy the earth? (Genesis 6:11-12) P6

Because of Sin

6. What did God tell Noah to make? (Genesis 6:14) P7

An Ark

7. What was the purpose of building this mode of transportation? (Genesis 6:17) P7

To be saved from the flood

8. How many pairs of clean animals was Noah to take? (Genesis 7:2) P7

2 of each kind

9. How old was Noah when he and his family entered the transportation? (7:6) P7

600

10. How long did the waters stay upon the earth? (Genesis 7:24) P8

40 Days

11. Noah was building a mode of transportation to save him and his family. How do you think others perceived it and what would you have done?

Perceive him as being Rediculas

Thought Question. *Has there ever been a time when you had to do something unpopular with others? Have there been times when people thought your decisions were crazy, but you knew they were of God? Think about it. How did you react? What was the outcome?*

3 ENOCH

1. Fill in the blanks. (Genesis 5:3 KJV)

   And Adam lived ~~an~~ 130 ~~~~~~ years, and begat a son in his own likeness, after his image; and called his name Seth.

2. Who was Enoch's father? (Genesis 5:18) P12

   Jared

3. How old was Enoch's father when he was born? (Genesis 5:18)

   162

4. How long did Enoch's father live after he was born? (Genesis 5:19)

   _800_

5. What was the total years that Enoch's father lived? (Genesis 5:20)

   _962_

6. Who was Enoch's son? (Genesis 5:21) P12

   Methuselah

7. How old was Enoch when his son was born? (Genesis 5:21)

   _65_

8. Fill in the blanks. (Genesis 5:22)

   And Enoch _walked_ with God after he begat _Methuselah_ three hundred years, and begat sons and daughters.

9. What were the total years that Enoch was on the earth? (Genesis 5:23) P12

   _365_

> **Thought Question.** What do you imagine it was like for a man of such integrity as Enoch in his days? Though his time on earth was short, it was amazing. What will you do to leave a lasting impression?

Generations From Adam to Noah

Genesis 5:3-24

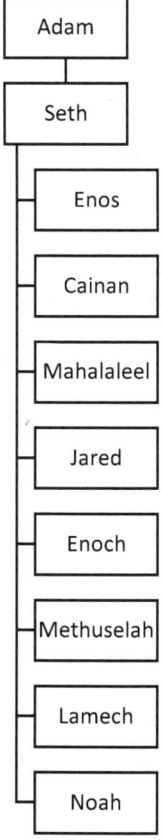

4 ABRAHAM

1. Circle the correct answer. Abraham was _____ P13

    a) "the friend of God"

    b) The father of the faithful

    c) The progenitor of the Israelites

    d) The first of the Hebrews

    e) (All of the above)

2. Where was Abraham born? (Genesis 11:31) P14

    __UR of The Caldees__

3. What was Abraham's father's name? (Genesis 11:31) P14

    __Terah__

4. Which son of Noah did Abraham's father descend from? (Genesis 11:10-31) P14

   Shem

5. What were the promises made to Abraham if he obeyed God, left his kindred, and traveled to the place God would show him? (Genesis 12:1-3) P14

   a. He would become a great nation
   b. God will make his name great
   c. He would be blessed
   d. He would be a blessing
   e. God will bless those that bless him and curse those that curse him
   f. All the families of the earth will be blessed in him
   g. And the land He tread on will be given to his descendants

6. By what name do we generally call these combined promises to Abraham? P15 (top of page)

   The Abrahamic Convenant

7. How old was Abraham when he left Haran? (Genesis 12:4b) P15

   75

8. Fill in the blank. (Genesis 15:6 KJV)

   And he believed in the LORD; and he counted it to him for _his high moral character_

> ***Thought Question.*** *Abraham was called to leave his brethren and go to a strange place where he had never been. That took faith and courage. Has there been a time when you had to leave a comfortable place? How did you feel about it? What was the outcome?*

Generations From Noah to Abraham

Genesis 1:10-31

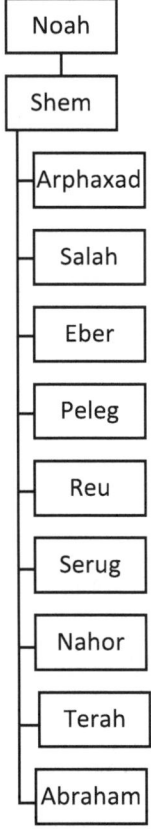

5 ISAAC

1. Fill in the blanks. (Genesis 21:2 KJV)

   For Sarah _Conceived_, and bare Abraham a son in his old age, at the _Exact_ time of which God had spoken to him.

2. Sarah and Abraham named their son Isaac. What does the name mean? P17

   Laughter

3. What covenant was Isaac heir to?

   Abrahamic Covenant

4. Circle the correct answer. How old was Isaac when he was circumcised? (Genesis 21:4) P18

   a. One year

   b. Two weeks

   c. Eight days

   d. Seven months

5. When his father thought he was taking Isaac to be offered as a sacrifice, what did the sacrificial Isaac carry? (Genesis 22:6) P19

6. What question did Isaac ask his father? (Genesis 22:7) P19

7. What did Isaac do when he saw his wife was barren? (Genesis 25:21) P20

> ***Thought Question.*** *Isaac's trust in his father was complete faith that he knew what was best and would take care of him. What does this teach us about our heavenly father?*

THE COVENANT OF CIRCUMCISION

This is my covenant, which ye shall keep, between me and you and thy seed after thee; Every man child among you shall be circumcised. And ye shall circumcise the flesh of your foreskin; and it shall be a token of the covenant betwixt me and you. And he that is eight days old shall be circumcised among you, every man child in your generations, he that is born in the house, or bought with money of any stranger, which is not of thy seed. He that is born in thy house, and he that is bought with thy money, must needs be circumcised: and my covenant shall be in your flesh for an everlasting covenant. And the uncircumcised man child whose flesh of his foreskin is not circumcised, that soul shall be cut off from his people; he hath broken my covenant. (Genesis 17:10-14 KJV)

6 JACOB

1. Fill in the blank. (Genesis 47:7 KJV) P21

   And Joseph brought in Jacob his father, and set him before Pharaoh: and Jacob _____ Pharaoh.

2. In the line of descent among the Hebrew patriarchs (the Hebrew Triumvirate), which place is Jacob? Circle the correct answer. P21, 22

   a. First

   b. Fifth

   c. Third

   d. Second

3. Why did Jacob and his brother struggle in their mother's womb? (Genesis 25:23) P21, 22

4. Who was firstborn, Jacob or his brother Esau? (Genesis 25:25)

   _____

5. How old was Isaac when his sons were born? (Genesis 25:26)

   _____

6. What does Jacob's name mean? P22

   _____

7. What did Jacob trick Esau into selling him for a bowl of pottage? (Genesis 25:29-34)

   _____

8. What did Jacob and his mother trick Isaac into doing? (Genesis Chapter 27) P21, 22

9. On his way to Padanaram, Jacob had a dream. What did he see? (Genesis 29:12-15) P22

10. Which sister did Jacob see first and fall madly in love with? (Genesis 30:9-11) P22

    _____

11. Jacob is the progenitor of the Twelve Tribes of Israel. How many of those twelve patriarchs did Leah give birth to? P22

    _____

12. After twenty years of serving his father-in-law, Jacob returned home to reconcile with Esau. On his way home, he had a dream. What did he see, and what happened? (Genesis 32:24-32) P23

13. What did Jacob's sons do in Shechem that caused Jacob to leave and go to Bethel? (Genesis 34:13-31) P24

14. Why did Jacob's older sons hate Joseph so much? (Genesis 37:3-4) P24

15. Fill in the blank. (Genesis 47:10 KJV) P21

    And Jacob _____ Pharaoh, and went out from before Pharaoh.

16. Fill in the blank. (Hebrews 7:7 KJV) P26

    And without all contradiction the less is _____ of the better.

> ***Thought Question.*** *Think about the life of this great patriarch, the progenitor of the Twelve Tribes of Israel. As you recall his life, what can you learn from him, both good and bad? How will that help you in your life or raising your children?*

THE GATES OF THE HOLY JERUSALEM

And he carried me away in the spirit to a great and high mountain, and shewed me that great city, the holy Jerusalem, descending out of heaven from God, Having the glory of God: and her light was like unto a stone most precious, even like a jasper stone, clear as crystal; And had a wall great and high, and had twelve gates, and at the gates twelve angels, and names written thereon, which are the names of the twelve tribes of the children of Israel: (Revelation 21:10-12 KJV)

THE TWELVE TRIBES OF ISRAEL

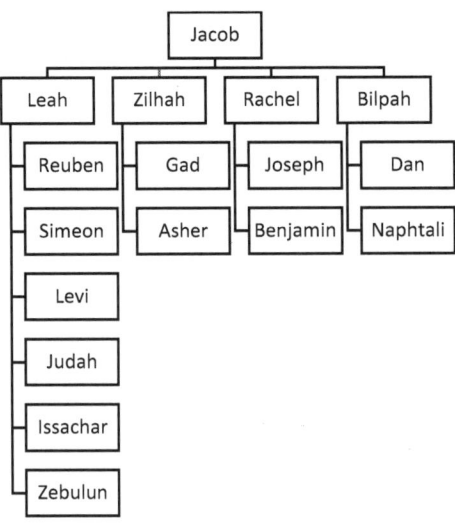

7 JOSEPH

1. How old was Joseph when his father sent him to check on his brothers? (Genesis 37:2) P28

   Seventeen

2. What did his brothers do to Joseph? (Genesis 37:19-28) P28, 29

   They put him in a pit then sold him to some Istmalites

3. What happened that Potiphar had Joseph put into prison? (Genesis 39:7-20) P29

   His wife Tricked into Thinking that Joseph Tried to Rape her (lie with her)

4. What was the interpretation of Pharaoh's dream? (Genesis 41:25-32) P29

Pharaoh would have seven years of plenty and seven years of famine. The dream was repeated twice because it would soon come to pass by God

5. How did Pharaoh honor Joseph for his interpretation? (Genesis 41:33-44) P29

You shall be over my house and all my people. Shall be ruled according to your word

6. What did Joseph's brothers think he might do when their father died? (Genesis 50:15-18) P30

That he might take vengeance upon them.

7. What did Joseph tell them? (Genesis 50:19-21)

Do not be afraid for I am in the place of God. You meant evil for me but God meant it for good. To save many people life

8. How old was Joseph when he died? (Genesis 50:22, 26)

110 years

9. What instructions had Joseph given for his burial? (Genesis 50:24-26) P30

That they will take his body to the promised land.

> **Thought Question.** Joseph was kind to his brothers after testing them to see if they had changed. Their reconciliation showed that relationships that seem permanently broken can be restored. Are there relationships in your life that need restoration? What do you plan to do about it?

8 JUDAH

1. What does the name Judah (Yehuda in Hebrew) mean? (Genesis 29:35) P31

   _____

2. Which son of Jacob's was Judah in the line of descent of the patriarchs? Circle the correct answer. P31

   a. Sixth

   b. Fourth

   c. First

   d. Seventh

3. What was his mother's name? (Genesis 29:32-35) P31

   _____

4. Why did Judah's daughter-in-law deceive him into impregnating her? (Genesis Chapter 38) P32, 33

5. What did Judah do when Jacob did not want to send Benjamin with his brothers to Egypt? (Genesis 43:8-9) P34

6. What did Judah do when Joseph had Benjamin taken into custody? (Genesis 44:16-34) P34, 35

7. What is the great prophetic blessing Jacob bestowed upon Judah, and what does it mean to us? (Genesis 49:8-12) P36

8. Fill in the blanks. (Revelation 5:5 KJV)

And one of the elders saith unto me, Weep not: behold, the _____ of the tribe of Juda, the _____ of David, hath prevailed to open the book, and to loose the seven seals thereof.

9. Fill in the blanks. (Revelation 22:16)

I Jesus have sent mine angel to testify unto you these things in the churches. I am the _____ and the _____ of David, and the bright and morning star.

Thought Question. *Judah was a patriarch in the Twelve Tribes of Israel and a predecessor of Christ. He was also a predecessor of David the King. His life shows God uses whom he pleases and that we can grow. How can you use Judah's life to live your own life?*

9 MOSES

1. Moses is a direct descendant of which Israelite patriarch? (Exodus 6:16-20) P37

   _____

2. Moses is considered the greatest prophet in which of the below religions? Circle the correct answer. P37

   a. Islam

   b. Christianity

   c. Judaism

   d. All of the above

2. Check the correct answer. Moses is considered by many scholars the greatest writer ever to have lived.

   ___ True   ___ False

3. Who was Moses' father? (Exodus 6:20)

    _____

4. Who was his mother? (Exodus 6:20) P38

    _____

5. Who are his famous siblings? (Numbers 26:59)

    _____   _____

6. Who adopted Moses? (Exodus 2:10) P38

    _____

7. Why did Moses flee Egypt? (Exodus 2:11-15) P38

8. Where did Moses flee to? (Exodus 2:15) P38

    _____

9. Who did Moses marry? (Exodus 2:21) P39

    _____

10. What was Moses doing when an angel of the Lord appeared to him, and he was called to lead Israel out of slavery? (Exodus 3:1-2) P39

11. When Moses asked who he should tell the children of Israel had sent him, what did God tell him to say? (Exodus 3:14)

12. Fill in the blanks. (Genesis 3:15 KJV)

And God said moreover unto Moses, Thus shalt thou say unto the children of Israel, The LORD God of your fathers, the God of _____, the God of _____, and the God of _____, hath sent me unto you: this is my name for ever, and this is my memorial unto all generations.

13. How long did the children of Israel wander in the wilderness? (Numbers 14:33) P39, 40

   _____

14. Why was Moses not allowed to enter the Promised Land? (Numbers 20:10-12) P41, 42, 43

Thought Question. *As a leader, as a man, and as a father, you will incur frustrations and setbacks. What lesson can you take from the leadership of Moses? How will you react?*

Notes

_____

_____

_____

_____

10 AARON

1. What office was Aaron the first to occupy? (Exodus 28:31) P46

   Great High Priest & Prophet of Lord

2. Who was older, Aaron or Moses? P46

   Aaron

3. What role did Aaron play in assisting Moses in delivering Israel from slavery in Egypt? (Exodus 4:14-16, 27-30) P47

   He was the spoke person to the people

4. What sin did Aaron commit while Moses was on Mt. Sinai receiving the commandments from the Lord? (Exodus 32:1-4) P47

Allowed them to build the golden calf.

5. Who influenced Aaron to rebel against the leadership of Moses? (Numbers 12:1-2) P47, 48

Miriam

6. Who was Aaron married to? (Exodus 6:23) P49

Jacobah Elishoba

7. What were the names of their sons? (Exodus 28:1) P48, 49

Nadab
Abihu
Eleazar
Ithamar

8. What were the Levites given to Aaron and his sons to do? (Numbers 18:6) P48

9. What did Aaron wear upon his head, and what was the inscription engraved on it? (Exodus 28:36-38) P50

Turban with a Medallion of Pure Gold and engrave it like a seal. then Attach it to the Turban.

10. Who is our Great High Priest? (Hebrews 4:15-16; 7:26-27) P50

Aaron Jesus

11. What is the date of Aaron's death? (Numbers 33:38) P52

123 years

12. How long did the congregation mourn for Aaron? (Numbers 20:29) P52

30 Days

Thought Question. *Aaron had many responsibilities. For the most part, he carried them out well. Like most men, he also had failures, struggles, and sorrows. Yet he had to lead the people. What lessons can you take from the life of Aaron?*

11 JOSHUA

1. What was the name of Joshua's father? (Exodus 33:11) P53

   Nun

2. What tribe was he from? (Numbers 13:8) P53

   Ephraim

3. When are we first introduced to Joshua in the Bible, and what was he chosen to do? (Exodus 17:1-14) P54

4. Circle the correct answer. What was Joshua's position? (Exodus 17:9, 24;13; Numbers 11:28, 27:16-23, Joshua 1:1-6) P53

   a) The General of Israel's armies ✓

   b) The servant of Moses

   c) The successor to Moses

   d) All of the above

5. Please check the correct answer. Joshua was one of the twelve men sent to spy on the Promised Land. True or false. (Numbers 13:8) P54

   ✓ True ___ False

6. Please check the correct answer. Joshua accompanied Moses to Mt. Sinai the first time he went to receive the Commandments. True or false. (Exodus 24:13) P54

   ✓ True ___ False

7. Fill in the blanks. (Numbers 34:17 KJV)

   These are the names of the men which shall divide the land unto you: __Eleazar__ the priest, and Joshua the son of __Nun__.

8. Fill in the blanks. (Joshua 1:9 KJV)

   Have not I commanded thee? Be __STRONG__ and of a good courage; be not __Afraid__, neither be thou dismayed: for the LORD thy God is with thee whithersoever thou goest.

9. How old was Joshua when he died? (Joshua 24:29) P56

   __110 years old__

10. Fill in the blanks. (Joshua 24) P56

    And if it seem evil unto you to __Serve__ the LORD, choose you this day whom ye will __Serve__; whether the gods which your fathers __Served__ that were on the other side of the flood, or the gods of the Amorites, in whose land ye dwell: but as for me and my house, we will __Serve__ the LORD.

> **Thought Question.** Joshua is an excellent example of leadership. What can you learn about leadership from his example?

To be faithful and obey God always.

12 CALEB

1. Caleb was one of twelve spies chosen to view the Promised Land and report back to the Children of Israel. Which tribe did he represent? (Numbers 13:6) P57

   Judah

2. Who was Caleb's father? (Numbers 14:30) P60

   Jephunneh

3. Ten of the men thought the giants in the land were too big to fight. What did Caleb report? (Numbers 13:30) P57

   They were too big to miss, and urged them to go up at once and take possesion of the land for we are well able to overcome.

4. The people turned against Moses and Aaron because they were frightened by the report of the ten negative men. What did Caleb and Joshua do and say? (Numbers 13:6-9) P59

Tore their clothes to show remorse and told them the land was good

5. Fill in the blanks. (Numbers 14:30 KJV) P60

Doubtless ye shall __not__ come into the land, concerning which I sware to make you dwell therein, save Caleb the son of __Save__, and Joshua the son of __Nun__.

6. How old was Caleb when Moses went the spies out to view the land? (Joshua 14:7)

__40__

7. How old was Caleb when he claimed his inheritance in the Promised Land on the day Joshua divided the lots? (Joshua 14:10)

__85__

8. Fill in the blanks. (Joshua 14:11 KJV) P61

As yet I am as __Strong__ this day as I was in the day that __Moses ~~Sent~~__ sent me: as my __Strength__ was then, even so is my __Strength__ now, for war, both to go out, and to come in.

9. Joshua blessed Caleb and assigned him what lot of land in the Promised Land? (Joshua 14:13-14) P61

__Hebron__

> **Thought Question.** Caleb maintained his faith in the Almighty God despite what his eyes saw and what others said. He stood for integrity. He stood for right. Have you ever had to stand even if you stood alone? Know that when you do, God stands with you.

Numbers chapter 14

13 SAMSON

1. Who was the father of Samson? (Judges 13:1) P62

   Manoah

2. What tribe was his father from? (Judges 13:1) P62

   Dan

3. What city did he live in? (Judges 13:1) P62

   Zorah

4. When the angel of the Lord appeared to Samson's mother, what instructions did he give her for raising Samson? (Judges 13:3-5) P63

   must not Drink wine, or any other alcohoic beverage Nor eat any forbidden fruit.

5. Where did Samson meet a woman of the Philistines that he wanted to marry? (Judges 14:1) P63

    A Philistine woman from Timnah

6. What riddle did Samson put to the thirty companions, and what did it mean? (Judges 14:5-14) P63, 64

    Out of the eater came forth meat and out the strong came forth sweetness.

7. Why did Samson cave in and tell his wife the riddle? (Judges 14:15-18) P64

    She cried, weeped and gave him the colder - the men had to threating to burn down her fathers house. He was physically strong but had a weak moral nature for women.

8. How long did Samuel judge Israel? (Judges 15:20) P66

    Twenty years

9. What happened when Samson went to see a harlot in Gaza? (Judges 16:1-3) P66

    Word soon spread that Samson was there, so the men of Gaza gathered together and waited all night at the town gates.

10. How did Delilah get Samson to reveal the source of his great strength? (Judges 16:15-17) P66, 67

    She tormented and nagged him and told him he did not love her.

11. The Philistines captured Samuel, put out his eyes, and made him labor, but what began to happen? (Judges 16:22) P68

    His hair began to grow back

12. Samson killed more people at his death than he had slain in his life. How did he kill them? (Judges 16:23-30) P68

    By asking the young servant to place his hands against the pillars that held up the temple. I wanted to push against them.

***Thought Question.** Samson was physically strong, but seemed to have a weakness for women. How can we love others and remain faithful to God?*

14 SAMUEL

1. Circle the correct answer. P69 Samuel was _____

    a. A major prophet

    b. A high priest

    c. The last judge who ruled Israel

    d. **All of the above**

2. Samuel's father, Elkanah, had two wives. Hannah was the mother of Samuel. What was the name of his other wife? (Samuel 1:2) P69

    Peninnah

3. What vow was Samuel under from his mother's womb? P69

    She vowed to give the back to the Lord

4. Why did Hannah name her child Samuel, and what does the name mean? (1 Samuel 1:20) P69

Heard of God or Name of God

5. Hannah vowed to give her son back to the Lord. When she was weaned, she took him and placed him in the service of the High Priest. Who was the High Priest at that time? (1 Samuel 1:24-25) P69, 70

Eli

6. Fill in the blanks. (1 Samuel 1:26 KJV) P70

For this child I __PRAYED__; and the LORD hath given me my __Petition__ which I asked of him.

7. What prophecy did God reveal to Samuel as a child? (1 Samuel 3:11-14) P70. 71

8. Fill in the blank. (1 Samuel 7:15 KJV)

And Samuel __Ruled__ Israel all the days of his life.

9. Samuel grew old, and his sons did not walk in his ways. The people demanded a king. Samuel was against it. What did the Lord say? (1 Samuel 8:7-9) P729. Do everything they say to you for the no longer want me for their King. They are rejecting me not you.

10. Why did the people demand a king be placed over them? (1 Samuel 8:19-20) P72, 73
They wanted to be like the world around them

11. Who did Samuel anoint to be the first king of Israel? (1 Samuel 9:15-17, 10:1) P73
Saul

12. What tribe was he from? (1 Samuel 9:1) P73
Benjamin

13. After the first king sinned and was rejected from being king, who did Samuel anoint to be the next king? (1 Samuel 16:13) P73
David

14. Where was Samuel buried? (1 Samuel 25:1) P73

His House in Ramah

> ***Thought Question.*** *Samuel and Eli before him were great prophets of the Lord, but their sons did not follow in their footsteps. What are your thoughts on this, and what will you do as a role model for other men following in your footsteps to help them stay on the right road?*

I would encourage them to obey God and do what the Lord's commandment says which is obey your parents

ELKANAH

Although Elkanah, Samuel's father, dwelled in Mount Ephraim, scripture verifies he was a Levite. The Levites had no inheritance in the Promised Land because they were set aside for service in the Temple but were given 48 cities throughout the land.

Now there was a certain man of Ramathaimzophim, of mount Ephraim, and his name was Elkanah, the son of Jeroham, the son of Elihu, the son of Tohu, the son of Zuph, an Ephrathite: (1 Samuel 1:1 KJV)

Elkanah is traced back to Levi through his son Kohath in 1 Chronicles 6:32-38.

Levi
Kohath
Izhar
Korah
Ebiasaph
Assir
Tahath
Zephaniah
Azariah
Joel
Elkahan I
Amasai
Mahath
Elkanah II
Zuph
Tohu
Eliel
Jeroham
Elkanah III
Samuel

It was originally created for "Forces to be Reckoned With: Formidable Women" Chapter 15, page 32, and used with the author's permission.

15 DAVID

1. Why did God have Samuel anoint David king of Israel? (1 Samuel 13:14) P75

2. Why did Saul's servants recommend he seek someone to play music for him? (1 Samuel 16:14-16) P76, 77

3. What instrument did David play? (1 Samuel 16:17-23) P76

4. Besides being a gifted musician, what other gifts did David have? P77

5. What did Saul promise as a reward to the man who would kill Goliath? (1 Samuel 17:25) P77

6. How did David kill Goliath? (1 Samuel 17:40-51) P78

7. What promise was made to David in what has become known as the Davidic Covenant? (2 Samuel 7:4-17) P79

8. What sin did David commit that precipitated him to write Psalms 51? (1 Samuel Chapter 11) P79

9. Who was the commander-in-chief of David's army? (1 Chronicles 27:34) P80

   _____

10. Who was set over David's personal guard? (2 Samuel 23:20-23) P82

    _____

11. What did David greatly desire to build for the Lord? (1 Chronicles 28:2-3) P83

12. Who succeeded David as king? (1 Chronicles 28:5) P83, 84

    _____

Thought Question. What do you see as David's greatest characteristic that made him the leader he was? What lesson can you take from David as a leader?

16 ELIJAH

1. Fill in the blank. P86

   Elijah the Tishbite is "one of the most _____ prophets in the Bible."

2. Elijah appears very suddenly on the stage of Bible History to deliver a hard message to King Ahab. What is the message he delivers? (1 Kings 1:2) P86, 87

3. The word of God came to him and told him to do what immediately after delivering the message? (1 Kings 1:3) P87

4. Who had God commanded to feed Elijah? (1 Kings 3:4) P87, 88

   _____

5. When his water source dried up, God sent Elijah to the house of a widow in Zarephath, a city of Zidon. What does the name "Zidon" mean? P88

   _____

6. What was the widow doing when Elijah arrived? (1 Kings 3:12) P88

7. What did Elijah ask her to do? (1 Kings 3:10-11) P88

8. What was the promise made to the widow? (1 Kings 17:13-14) P88

9. The woman's son fell ill and died sometime later. What miracle did Elijah perform that is the first of its kind in the Bible? (1 Kings 17:17-22) P89

10. What does the word "Zarephath" mean? P90

   _____

11. After the showdown with Jezebel's prophets, where did Ahab run to escape Jezebel's wrath, and where did he sit? (1 Kings 19:3-4) P92, 93

12. Who brought him food there twice? (1 Kings 19:5-7) P93

13. How long did Elijah go on the strength of that food? (1 Kings 19:8) P93

    _____

14. Who did Elijah anoint to succeed him as chief of the prophets? (1 Kings 19:16) P94

    _____

15. Can you describe how Elijah was translated? (2 Kings 2:1-2) P96

Thought Question. *What did Elijah do that all successful leaders must do? How can you incorporate some of Elijah's acts into your own realm?*

17 JONADAB

1. Jonadab was the son of whom? (2 Kings 10:15) P100

   _____

2. What does his name mean? P100

3. Which people was he descended from? (1 Chronicles 2:55) P100, 101

   _____

4. Jonadab rode in the chariot with Jehu to Samaria. What did they do there? (2 Kings 10:17) P101

5. What did God command Jeremiah to do with the Rechabites? (Jeremiah 35:1-5) P102

6. What did Jonadab command his children and their descendants to do? (Jeremiah 35:6-7) P101

7. Some 250 years later, God tested the Rechabite's obedience to Jonadab. What was the reason? (Jeremiah 35:16-17) P102

8. Explain the test and the results of it. (Jeremiah 35:2-6) P102, 103

9. What commendation and promise was given to the Rechabites for their unwavering obedience to their father? (Jeremiah 35:18-19)

> ***Thought Question.*** *Jonadab is an outstanding example of a faithful man of God passing his faith down to his children after him. What lessons can you take from his life and use to pass your faith down to future generations?*

Notes

_____

_____

_____

_____

18 JOB

1. Where did Job live? (Job 1:1) P106

   _____

2. Circle the correct answer. (Job 1:1) P106

   Job was _____

   a. Perfect and upright

   b. Mean and ornery

   c. Small of stature

3. How many sons did Job have? (Job 1:2) P107

   _____

4. How many daughters did Job have? (Job 1:2) P107

   _____

5. What was Job's substance, or what was the amount of his wealth? (Job 1:3) P107

6. How do we know Job was concerned about his children and their relationship with God? (Job 1:4-5) P108

7. God held Job up as an example of righteousness to Satan. What did Satan say about that? (Job 1:9-11) P109

8. Job was tested twice. What was his first test? (Job 1:13-19) P110-112

9. How did Job respond to this test? (Job 1:20-22) P112

10. In Job's second test, his skin was afflicted with an indescribable illness. What did his wife tell him he should do, and how did he respond? (Job 2:9-10)

11. Who were the friends that came to sit with him? (Job 2:11) P113

12. Job's friends gave a series of speeches that did not comfort him. What did he call them? (Job 16:2) P114, 115

   _____

13. God turned Job's situation around. What did Job have to do for his friends? (Job 42:5-10) P117

14. What was Job's "latter end?" (Job 42:12-13) P117

15. What did Job do for his daughters that was unusual? (Job 42:15) P118

16. How long does the Bible say Job lived after this? Job 42:16) P118

   _____

17. How many generations of his descendants did he see? (Job 42:16) P118

   _____

Thought Question. Job was a blameless man who loved his family and brought his children up to worship the one true God. He did everything right, and yet he was severely tried. His example is that he endured the trials and was blessed doubly at the end. How can you apply Job's example to your life?

19 DANIEL

1. In what year of the reign of Jehoiakim, king of Judah, did Nebuchadnezzar, king of Babylon, besiege Jerusalem? (Daniel 1:1) P120

   _____

2. What did Nebuchadnezzar do with part of the vessels of the house of God? (Daniel 1:2) P120, 121

3. Who was the master of the eunuchs in Nebuchadnezzar's administration? (Daniel 1:3) P122

   _____

4. Nebuchadnezzar took the best and brightest children of noble birth to train for work in his administration. What four children were among them? (Daniel 1:6) P121

5. Why did Daniel and his friends refuse the king's food? (Daniel 1:8) P122

7. Who was the prince of the eunuchs set over David and his friends? (Daniel 1:11) P123

   _____

8. How did Daniel and his friends do when the king tested them? (Daniel 1:17-20) P124

9. How was Daniel given the interpretation of Nebuchadnezzar's first dream? (Daniel 2:19) P127

10. What was the interpretation of Nebuchadnezzar's second dream? (Daniel 4:24-26) P131, 132

11. What was Belshazzar doing when he saw the fingers of a man's handwriting on the wall? (Daniel 5:1-5)

12. What was the interpretation of the message on the wall? (Daniel 5:25-28)? P134, 135

13. Why did the other administrators seek to find fault in Daniel? (Daniel 6:1-5) P136

14. God kept Daniel safe in the lion's den, but what happened to his accusers? (Daniel 6:24) P138

Thought Question. *Daniel is a great example of excellence. He kept his faith under all circumstances. His life was dynamic because he held to his principles. What can you take from the life of this great prophet and apply in your own life?*

20 THE THREE HEBREW BOYS

1. Nebuchadnezzar caused a massive image of gold to be made. How big was it? (Daniel 3:1) P140

2. Nebuchadnezzar summoned all his officials to the dedication of the statue. What were they commanded to do at the sound of the music? (Daniel 3:5) P141

3. What would be the penalty for those who disobeyed this command? (Daniel 3:6) P141

4. Shadrach, Meshach, and Abednego did not obey the command. Who ratted them out? (Daniel 3:8) P141, 142

5. How did they respond to the king's ultimatum? (Daniel 3:16-18) P142, 143

6. As a result of his rage, what did Nebuchadnezzar do? (Daniel 3:19-20) P143

7. What happened to the men who threw them in? (Daniel 3:22) P143

8. Nebuchadnezzar, the King, was astonished at the sight he saw. What did he see? (Daniel 3:24-25) P143

9. What decree did the king issue after this miraculous deliverance of the three Hebrew boys? (Daniel 3:28-29) P143, 144

10. What did he do for the three Hebrew boys? (Daniel 3:30) P144

***Thought Question.** The three Hebrew boys defied the king and all odds by refusing to worship an idol god. Can you recall a time when you had to defy authority for your faith? What was the outcome?*

21 ZACHARIAS

1. Who was King of Judea when Zacharias was ministering as a priest? (Luke 1:5) P145

   _____

2. What does the name Zacharias mean? P145

   _____

3. What course or lot did Zacharias minister in? (Luke 1:5) P145

4. Who was Zacharias married to? (Luke 1:5) P145

   _____

5. What tribe were they descended from? (Luke 1:5) P146

   _____

6. Circle the correct answer. (Luke 1:6) P146

   "They were _____"

   a. Both righteous before God

   b. Walking in all the commandments and ordinances of the Lord

   c. Blameless

   d. All of the above

7. An angel appeared to Zacharias one day while he was ministering in the temple. What announcement did the angel make? (Luke 1:11-17) P147

8. What was the name of the angel? (Luke 1:19)

   _____

9. Zacharias asked for a sign. What sign was he given? (Luke 1:20) P148

> ***Thought Question.*** *Zacharias was given a sign, but it was not a good sign. Sometimes, God has to keep us silent to perform his work. Can you recall a time when you spoke too soon or spoke without thinking? Perhaps there has been a time when you said something rashly and regretted it. What will you do in the future?*

Notes

_____
_____
_____
_____
_____
_____

22 JOSEPH OF NAZARETH

1. According to the book of Matthew, how many generations are there from Abraham to David? (Matthew 1:17)

   14

2. According to the book of Matthew, how many generations are there from David until the carrying away into Babylon? (Matthew 1:17)

   14

3. According to the book of Matthew, how many generations are there from the carrying away unto Christ? (Matthew 1:17)

   14

4. Joseph was engaged to Mary when she conceived of the Holy Spirit. While Joseph was wondering what to do, who appeared to him in a dream? (Matthew 1:20) P153

An Angel of the Lord

5. What did the angel tell Joseph? (Matthew 1:20-23) P153 Not to be afraid to take Mary as his wife for the child within her was conceived by the Holy Spirit

6. What did Joseph do when he arose from his sleep? (Matthew 1:24-25) P154 He did as the angel told him. He married her, but he never touched her until her son was born.

Thought Question. *Joseph is unusual. He married Mary and was given the responsibility of raising the Christ Child. Because of his faith, he is revered by Christians everywhere. What can you do for a better generation of young men, even if they are not your sons?*

Notes

23 SIMEON

1. Circle the correct answer. (Luke 2:25) P155

   Simeon _____

   a. Was just and devout

   b. Was waiting for the consolation of Israel

   c. The Holy Ghost was upon him

   d. All of the above

2. Why did Mary and Joseph bring Jesus to the temple? (Luke 2:22-23) P155

3. What had been revealed to Simeon? (Luke 2:26) P158

4. Simeon praised God. Who did he bless? (Luke 2:34) P159

5. What did Simeon say the child was "set" for? (Luke 2:34) P159

> ***Thought Question.*** *Simeon waited all his life for The Messiah. He could wait because it was revealed to him that he would not die before he saw him. Is there something God has promised you to see in your life? Wait on it. He is as sure as his word.*

24 JOHN THE BAPTIST

1. Who was the father of John the Baptist, and what was his office? (Luke 1:5, 8, 13, 62, 63) P160

2. Who was the mother of John the Baptist? (Luke 1:5, 13, 24, 57, 60) P160

3. What special instructions were given to his father concerning his birth and how he would be raised? (Luke 1:13-17) P160

1 ADAM

1. On what day of creation did God create man? (Genesis 1:31)

2. Fill in the blanks. (Genesis 1:26 KJV) P1

   And God said, Let us make _____ in our _____, after our _____: and let them have _____ over the fish of the sea, and over the fowl of the air, and over the cattle, and over all the earth, and over every creeping thing that creepeth upon the earth.

4. John was born only months before Jesus. Based on the age of Jesus when he entered into ministry, how old was John when he entered into ministry? (Luke 3:23a) P161

5. What was the message of John the Baptist? (Matthew 3:1-3) P162

6. What did John say when he saw Jesus coming to the river where he was baptizing? (John 1:29) P163

7. When John baptized Jesus, what seal of the Father was seen? (Matthew 3:14-17) P163

8. Who did John reprove for having his brother's wife? (Luke 3:19-20) P164

9. How did Herodias trick her husband into having John beheaded? (Matthew 14:6-8) P164, 165

10. Fill in the blanks. (Luke 7:28) KJV) P165

    For I say unto you, Among those that are born of _____ there is not a _____ prophet than John the Baptist: but he that is _____ in the kingdom of God is greater than he.

Thought Question. John the Baptist was the forerunner of Jesus. He was a great man but said he was unworthy to baptize Jesus. His humility and faith should serve as a lesson to all of us. His reproof of Herod upset Herodias. Have there been times in your life that you had to reprove someone? What was the result?

25 THE APOSTLES

1. What power did Jesus give to twelve of his disciples? (Matthew 10:1) P167

2. What does the word "Apostle" mean? (Matthew 10:5) P166

3. Please name the original twelve apostles. (Matthew 10:2-4) P166

_____ _____

_____ _____

_____ _____

_____ _____

_____ _____

_____

4. To whom were the first twelve apostles sent? (Matthew 10:5-6) P167

5. Jesus later appointed other disciples. How many did he appoint the second time? (Luke 10:1-2) P167

_____

6. What was Andrew and Simon's (Peter) relationship? (John 1:40-42) P167

_____

7. What was Andrew and Simon's occupation? (Matthew 4:18) P167, 168

   _____

8. James and John were brothers. Who was their father? (Matthew 4:21) P168

   _____

9. What surname did Jesus refer to James and John by, and what does it mean? (Mark 3:17) P169

10. What was Matthew's occupation? (Matthew 9:9) P171

    _____

11. Where do we get the phrase "Doubting Thomas" from? (John 20:20) P171

12. How did Judas Iscariot die? (Matthew 27:5) P172

13. What criteria did the disciples use to choose a replacement for the apostleship of Judas Iscariot? (Acts 1:21-22) P172

14. Who was chosen to replace Judas? (Acts 1:26) P173

   _____

Thought Question. *The apostles were regular men with regular occupations, yet they were chosen for greatness. Many were martyred. What can you learn from their lives?*

26 NICODEMUS

1. What sect of the Jews was Nicodemus? (John 3:1) P176

   _____

2. True or false. Nicodemus was a ruler of the Jews. (John 3:1) P176

   ___ True   ___ False

3. Check the correct answer. (John 3:2) P177

   Nicodemus came to Jesus _____

   a. By night

   b. By day

   c. By highway

4. What did Nicodemus say to Jesus when he first approached him? (John 3:2) P177

5. How did Jesus answer Nicodemus? (John 3:3) P178

6. What question did Nicodemus ask after Jesus answered him? (John 3:4) P179

7. What does Jesus' answer to Nicodemus' second question mean in your own words? (John 3:5) P179, 180

***Thought Question.** Though Nicodemus may not have fully understood what Jesus taught then, he seemed to have embraced his teachings at the last. Sometimes, we witness to people and they don't fully seem to understand. What should we do in such a case?*

27 THE NOBLEMAN

1. Where was Jesus when the nobleman found him? (John 4:46) P182

   _____

2. Where was the nobleman from? (John 4:46) P182

   _____

3. The nobleman sought Jesus to heal his sick son. How did Jesus first respond? (John 4:48) P182, 183

4. What did the nobleman say after Jesus responded? (John 4:49) P183

5. How did Jesus answer this time? (John 4:50) P183

6. As the nobleman journeyed home, his servants met him. What did they say? (John 4:51) P183

7. This confirmed the faith of the nobleman. What were the consequences of his faith? (John 4:53) P183

Thought Question. Hopeless though the situation seemed, the nobleman sought and received help in his desperate time. What hope does that give you for your desperate times?

28 THE ROMAN CENTURION

1. Where was Jesus when the Roman centurion approached him? (Luke 7:1) P184

   _____

2. How is the servant's relationship to the Roman centurion described? (Luke 7:2) P184

3. Why did the Jewish elders beg Jesus to heal the servant, and why is it rare that a Jew would commend a Roman centurion? (Luke 7:3-5) P185

4. What did the Roman centurion say when Jesus said he would come and heal his servant? (Matthew 8:8-9) P185, 186

5. In your own words, describe the principle of authority presented in this case. (Matthew 8:8-9) P186, 187

6. What great commendation did Jesus make about the Roman Centurion? (Matthew 8:10, Luke 7:9) P187, 189

7. When was the servant healed? (Matthew 8:13) P188

Thought Question. Do men of great authority recognize others with authority? Do you recognize others?

29 JAIRUS

1. Who, or what occupation, was Jairus? (Luke 8:41) P189

   _____

2. His daughter was sick. What did he do when he saw Jesus? (Matthew 9:18, Luke 8:42) P189, 190

3. What interrupted Jesus on his way to Jairus' house? (Matthew 9:20-22, Luke 8:43-48) P191

4. What did Jesus say when someone came from Jairus' house saying his daughter was dead? (Luke 8:50) P191

5. What did Jesus do with the naysayers and scorners when he arrived at the house? (Mark 5:40-42) P192

6. What did Jesus do and say when he entered the room where the child was lying? (Mark 5:40-42) P192

7. What did the child do? (Mark 5:40-42) P192

Thought Question. *Jairus believed and had his daughter restored. What will you do with the naysayers and pessimists when you encounter them?*

30 ZACCHAEUS

1. What was Zacchaeus' position among the tax collectors? (Luke 19:2) P193

2. Circle the correct answer. (Luke 19:2) P193

    Zacchaeus was _____

    a. poor

    b. rich

    c. moderate

3. Who are the publicans equivalent to in our time? (Luke 19:2) P193

    _____

4. Why did Zacchaeus have to climb a tree to see Jesus? (Luke 19:3-4) P194

5. What did Jesus say when passing the tree where Zacchaeus was? (Luke 19:5) P194

6. How did the crowd react? (Luke 19:7) P195

7. When Zacchaeus repented and promised to make restoration to anyone he had harmed, what did Jesus say? (Matthew 19:9-10) P195

Thought Question. *Zacchaeus repented and promised restoration to those he had harmed. What does that teach us about our own repentance?*

31 STEPHEN

1. On the day of Pentecost, the Holy Ghost ushered in and sat upon the disciples. What did it do for them? (Acts 2:4 P196

2. Who were the early church leaders? (Acts 6:2) P196

   _____

3. What murmurings arose among the Grecian or Hellenistic Jews? (Acts 6:1) P196, 197

4. What seven men of honest report were chosen and set over the business? (Acts 6:5) P197

   _____ _____

   _____ _____

   _____ _____

   _____

5. Fill in the Blanks. (Acts 6:8 KJV) P197

   And Stephen, full of _____ and _____, did great wonders and miracles among the people.

6. What accusations did false witnesses bring against Stephen? (Acts 6:8-14) P197

7. Briefly, what did Stephen include in his powerful defense of the gospel? (Acts 6:2-53) P198

8. What did the people do in response? (Acts 6:54) P198

9. What did Stephen do in response to their anger? (Acts 6:55-56) P198

10. Who was there consenting when the people stoned Stephen? (Acts 6:57-58) P199

_____

11. What did Stephen say and do when he was being stoned? (Acts 6:59-60) P199

Thought Question. People will not always agree with our witness. Some may react violently. What would you have done if faced with a situation similar to that of Stephen?

32 PHILIP

1. What did Philip do in Samaria? (Acts 8:5) (P201, 202

2. How did the people respond? (Acts 8:6-8) P202

3. When the apostles heard what happened in Samaria, what did they send Peter and John to do? (Acts 8:14-17) P203

4. When Simon, the sorcerer, saw what they had done, what did he do? (Acts 8:18-19) P203

5. What was Peter's response? (Acts 8:20-23) P203

6. Who told Philip to arise and go south from Jerusalem to Gaza? (Acts 8:26) P203

_____

7. Who did Philip see when he went, and what was he doing? (Acts 8:27-28) P203

8. What did Philip do? (Acts 8:35) P204

9. What did the man ask Philip when he had finished? (Acts 8:36) P204

10. Who stayed at Philip's home during one of his journeys? (Acts 21:8) P205

   _____

11. How many daughters did Philip have? (Acts 21:9) P205

   _____

12. What was their office, or what gift did they have? (Acts 21:9) P205

Thought Question. *Philip was a deacon who became an evangelist. We are all able to tell someone about Christ. It is the Clarion Call for every Christian. How do you witness to others?*

33 PAUL

1. What was Paul's claim to apostleship in your own words? (Galatians 1:1) P203

2. What is Paul's name in Hebrew? (Acts 7:58) P206

   _____

3. Whose death was Paul found consenting to? (Acts 7:58, 8:1, 22:20) P206, 207

   _____

4. In your own words, describe Paul's conversion experience on the road to Damascus. (Acts 9:1-8, 26:12-18) P207, 208, 209

5. What was Ananias' first reaction when the Lord sent him to Paul? (Acts 9:10-14) P209

6. What did the Lord tell him about Paul's future? (Acts 9:15-16) P209

7. What did Paul do right after his conversion? (Galatians 1:15-19) P210

8. Give just one reason why Paul's conversion is so important in the history of Christianity. P210

9. What day after his birth was Paul circumcised on? (Philippians 3:5) P210, 211

   _____

10. What tribe was Paul descended from? (Philippians 3:5) P210, 211

    _____

11. What sect of the Jews was Paul before his conversion? (Philippians 3:5) P210, 211

    _____

12. Where was Paul born? (Acts 22:3) P211

    _____

13. What well-known Hebrew teacher was he brought up at the feet of? (Acts 22:3) P211

    _____

14. True or false. Paul was a Roman citizen. (Acts 22:25-28) P211

    ___ True   ___ False

> ***Thought Question.*** *Paul was always zealous for whatever cause he believed. Whatever he did, he did it with all his might. What makes a man zealous? Is there anything that you do with all your might? How might you apply the principles that ruled Paul to your own life?*

BIBLE BOOKS WRITTEN BY PAUL	
BOOK	APPROXIMATE TIME
Galatians	49 AD-53 AD
1 Thessalonians	50 AD-51 AD
2 Thessalonians	51 AD-52 AD
1 Corinthians	55 AD-56 AD
2 Corinthians	55 AD-57 AD
Romans	56 AD-57 AD
Ephesians	60 AD-63 AD
Philippians	60 AD-63 AD
Philemon	60 AD-63 AD
Colossians	60 AD-63 AD
1 Timothy	62 AD-64 AD
Titus	62 AD-64 AD
2 Timothy	66 AD-67 AD

It is unknown if Paul wrote the Book of Hebrews, but if so, it was most likely written anytime between 61 AD and 67 AD.

Notes

BOOKS BY JEWEL HAMPTON

Genesis: The Greatest Love of All

Genesis: The Greatest Love of All Workbook

Exodus: The Power and the Glory

Exodus: The Power and the Glory Workbook

Forces to be Reckoned With: Formidable Women

Workbook Forces to be Reckoned With: Formidable Women

Forces to be Reckoned With: Formidable Men

Workbook Forces to be Reckoned With: Formidable Men

Made in the USA
Columbia, SC
27 June 2024

37775833R00065